CUBS in the TUB

The True Story of the Bronx Zoo's First Woman Zookeeper

CANDACE FLEMING

ILLUSTRATIONS BY JULIE DOWNING

NEAL PORTER BOOKS

HOLIDAY HOUSE/NEW YORK

Helen and Fred Martini longed
for a baby.
A baby to bottle-feed and burp.
A baby to rock and soothe and croon
lullabies to.
A baby to love with all their hearts.

Every morning, Fred went off to his job at the Bronx Zoo.

Helen stayed home to dream

and plan.

But still there was no baby. Until . . .

Fred explained. The mother
lion had lost the instinct to
take care of her baby.
She wouldn't feed him.
She wouldn't clean him.

She refused to even
look at him.

Helen cradled the baby close. She marveled at the tiny buds of his ears and the tender, pink undersides of his toes.

The first thing MacArthur needed
was a bath.
Good thing Helen had a baby tub.
She sang a lullaby as she sponged
his fur. Soon he was as fluffy
and soft as a lamb.

MacArthur gave
a husky cry.
Good thing she had
those baby bottles
and all those cans
of formula milk.
MacArthur slurped.

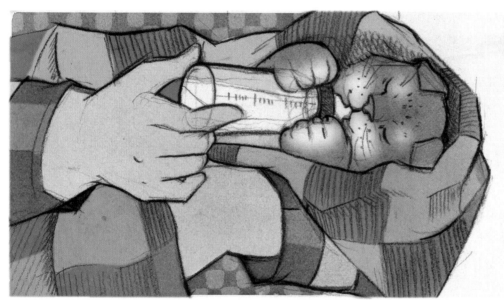

Then . . . UUURP!
A gentle pat on his back
brought up the bubbles
in his belly. With a
sigh, the baby snuggled
his downy head into the
curve of Helen's neck.
His sweet breath warmed her skin.

Tiptoeing to the crib—
good thing she had one—
she tucked him in.
Curling his little legs
beneath him,
MacArthur dreamed.

11

And grew.

Helen kept a record
of his "firsts."

A soft blue

On their eleventh day together, MacArthur opened his eyes.

On their fifteenth day together, he got his first tooth.

A needle-sharp incisor

And on their twenty-first day together, he took his first stumbling steps.

A great day!

13

Soon MacArthur was pouncing at Helen's ankles, chewing on Fred's boots, and leaping into their laps whenever either of them sat.

What joy it was to have
a baby in the house!

But when MacArthur was
two months old, officials
decided to send him to a
zoo in another city.

Helen held her baby close
until the car came.
And tried to smile as
MacArthur was driven away.

Then she folded up the baby
blankets; stowed tub, crib,
and bottles; and sank into
the rocking chair with empty
arms and an empty lap.

Gray day
followed
gray day.

Until . . .

Good thing she had
a heating pad.
She slipped it beneath
their tiny bodies, and
turned it to high.
Then she mixed a batch of
warm formula and squeezed
it into their mouths.
Drip. Drop. Drip.
One . . . two . . . three
babies began to wiggle.
The kitchen filled with
the faint chorus of high-
pitched cries.

She named them Raniganj,
Dacca, and Rajpur.

And once they
started eating,

they could not stop.

Every three hours.

Around the clock. Good thing Helen had Fred to help with those 2 a.m. feedings.

By the end of the first week, the babies had doubled their weight to four pounds.

Days passed. Blue eyes opened, and folded ears perked up.

Little teeth poked through pink gums.

Personalities appeared.

Raniganj cried whenever Helen put him down, and bit and scratched when he didn't get his way.

Dacca was forever boxing her brothers' faces with her fat little paws, then rolling on top of them, and pinning them down.

Rajpur liked to sleep. Good-naturedly, he accepted whatever came his way . . . especially food.

Helen let them get away with all
sorts of mischief.

They romped and tumbled. They
snuggled and purred.

What a joy it was to have three
babies in the house.

When the car came for them, Helen
climbed in. Her babies needed her.

At the zoo, she turned the glass-paneled cage into a cozy home. Blankets. Bottles. Boxes of toys. Good thing Helen brought them all. Then peeking around the partition, she watched her babies play. She called them back for naps and snacks and cuddles.

That night when the visitors left the zoo, the cubs sensed that Helen was leaving too. Raniganj cried.

Dacca clung to her ankles.

And Rajpur scrambled up into Helen's arms and wrapped his paws around her neck.

Refusing to stay in their cribs, the three struggled against sleep.

It was midnight before Helen finally tiptoed home.

In her own bed,
she tossed

and turned.

She imagined she heard
her babies crying.

At first light, she
rushed back to the zoo.

Her little ones were still
curled up, fast asleep.

She kissed one . . . two . . . three sleepy
cubs awake. Then it was bottles.

Baths.
Time to play.

Fred showed her the storeroom.
In secret and between bottles
and baths,

Helen cleaned,

painted,

decorated,

and
created . . .

a nursery!
Good thing Helen had all
that baby equipment.
That first night the babies
sniff-sniffed at the pink
ceiling and pale blue walls,
the ruffled curtains, the
cribs and toys. Then
snuggling close to
Helen, they purred.

Now the cubs spent their days in the glass-paneled cage. But they spent their nights with Helen in the nursery.

News of the nursery reached zoo officials. They stormed through the door . . . and stopped dead in their tracks. Helen raised her chin. "My babies need me." The officials looked at one another.

"So they do," agreed Mr. Crandall, the zoo curator. And he offered her the job of "keeper of the nursery." Helen was delighted. And surprised. Only men had held zookeeper jobs.

Until now.

Helen had mothered her way into becoming the first woman zookeeper at the Bronx Zoo.

She and her nursery stayed.

The babies grew.
Too big for laps.
Too big for cribs.
Too big for the nursery.

Officials moved them to
a larger, outdoor enclosure . . .
without Helen. They worried
the ten-month old tigers
would hurt her.

Nonsense. Even though they
were twice her size, Helen
argued, they still "run to me
for protection and comfort."

But zoo officials were firm.
Helen would never again
be allowed to enter the
tigers' cage.

Pressed against the outside of
the bars, her arms felt empty.

But not for long.
What a happy zoo family!

45

A QUIETER KIND OF HERO

Helen Martini really did establish a nursery for her tiger cubs in a storeroom of the Bronx Zoo's Lion House in 1944. By that time, she'd had three years of experience taking care of zoo babies, beginning with the arrival of MacArthur the lion cub. Nowadays, zoos carefully follow exact care and diet instructions for their animals based on veterinary science. Back then, zoos did not always know how to care for their animals. This helps explain why officials at the Bronx Zoo allowed Fred to bring the babies home to his wife. They simply didn't know what else to do. Luckily, for them, Helen did. According to her, she used "common sense and intuition" when caring for her babies, hitting on a diet of "evaporated milk and water heated to body temperature every three hours." Later she added chopped meat with bone meal, along with cod liver oil. At three months, she added chunks of meat. And for the first year, she administered liquid vitamins.

Her zoo nursery not only allowed Helen to be with her cubs, but it eventually led to a new career. In those days, "men ruled supreme in the zoo world," recalled Helen. "Caring for [the] animals had always been a man's job." But with the success of the nursery, zoo officials offered her a position. "I had sneaked in the back door," she confessed.

This is how women in Helen's day often

went about carving out opportunities for themselves. Back then, society expected women to stick to the traditional roles of wife and mother. But many women bucked these expectations. They weren't loud. They didn't call attention to themselves. Instead, with daring and cleverness, they subtly worked within the existing power structure. And they brought about change. They took strides. They accomplished firsts.

Helen Martini became the Bronx Zoo's first woman zookeeper.

And she was indispensable. In her two decades as the "animal nursery keeper," she cared for hundreds of babies, including a chimpanzee, two orangutans, three gorillas, a ring-tailed lemur, a pair of ocelots, a skunk, a sea lion, a litter of common marmosets, a round-tailed ground squirrel, an addax, a sika deer, and a long-eared hedgehog from Cyprus. The nursery, admitted Helen, often looked "like Noah's ark."

As for Raniganj, Dacca, and Rajpur, they continued to live at the Bronx Zoo. Helen and Fred oversaw their care, tickling them through the bars and celebrating their birthdays with "chopped meat cakes." The tigers never displayed any ferocity, although once when Helen's back was turned to the cage, Rajpur did creep up on her like he used to do as a baby. But now his gesture of affection was too much for her. Leaping, then rolling, his 450 pounds hit the bars with such force that he sent his foster mother sprawling.

Busy as she was at the zoo, she continued to raise cubs in her apartment on Old Kingsbridge Road. Over the years, she mothered five more tigers, and two more lions, as well as a panther and a pair of jaguars. Time and again, wrote Helen, her home "echoed to the infant cries of cats."

For a glimpse of Helen in her zoo nursery check out this Youtube video, Baby Gorilla (1951): www.youtube.com/watch?v=6RZF6DZ3-6E

SELECTED BIBLIOGRAPHY

"Introducing Princeton." *Princeton Alumni Weekly,* 14 October, 1949: 5.

Leen, Nina. "Zoo Season in the Sun," *Life Magazine,* 22 April, 1957: 73–76.

Martini, Helen. *My Zoo Family.* New York: Harper & Brothers, 1953.

Reiche, Bill. "Mothering the Zoo Babies." *Popular Mechanics Magazine,* August, 1947: 132–134.

SOURCE NOTES

p. 6   "Just do for him . . .": Martini, 6.

p. 8   "MacArthur. I'll name you": ibid.

p. 13   "A soft blue": ibid., 19.

p. 13   "A needle-sharp incisor": ibid.

p. 13   "A great day!": ibid., 9.

p. 20   "They're in a . . .": ibid., 17.

p. 28   "It's time for the cubs . . .": *Princeton Alumni Weekly*, 5.

p. 36   "Is there an . . .": ibid., 31.

p. 39   "My babies need me.": *Princeton Alumni Weekly*, 5.

p. 39   "So they do.": ibid.

p. 42   "run to me . . .": Martini, 41.

p. 46   "common sense . . .": Reiche, 133.

p. 46   "evaporated milk . . .": ibid.

p. 46   "men ruled supreme . . .": Martini, 34.

p. 46   "Caring for [the] . . .": ibid.

p. 46   "I had sneaked . . .": ibid.

p. 46   "animal nursery keeper": Leen, 73.

p. 46   "like Noah's ark.": Martini, 70.

p. 47   "chopped meat cakes.": ibid., 67.

p. 47   "echoed to the . . .": ibid., 208.

To mothers everywhere who fiercely protect their cubs —C.F.

*To my mother, who raised her own ambush of cubs
with such love and care —J.D.*

Neal Porter Books

Text copyright © 2020 by Candace Fleming
Illustrations copyright © 2020 by Julie Downing
All Rights Reserved
HOLIDAY HOUSE is registered in the U.S. Patent and Trademark Office.
Printed and bound in August 2021 at Toppan Leefung, Dong Guan City, China.
The artwork for this book was created with watercolor and colored pencils.
Book design by Jennifer Browne
www.holidayhouse.com
First Edition
3   5   7   9   10   8   6   4   2

Library of Congress Cataloging-in-Publication Data

Names: Fleming, Candace, author. | Downing, Julie, illustrator.
Title: Cubs in the tub : the true story of the Bronx Zoo's first woman
keeper / Candace Fleming ; illustrated by Julie Downing.
Description: New York : Holiday House, 2020. | "Neal Porter Books." |
Includes bibliographical references. | Audience: Ages 4-8 | Audience:
Grades 2-3 | Summary: "Readers are told the story of Helen Martini's
care for lion and tiger cubs, and her emergence as the Bronx Zoo's first
woman zookeeper" — Provided by publisher.
Identifiers: LCCN 2019032421 | ISBN 9780823443185 (hardcover)